Moira Butterfield

Ro Ledesma

STAR, Moon, ZOOM!

happy yak

CONTENTS

ABOUT THIS SPACE BOOK

Meet some kids and a very brainy dog called Charlie. They're here to help you find out more about our solar system and beyond.

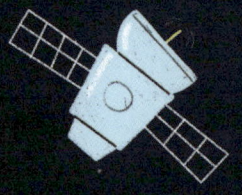

Oooh!

Aaaah!

Space looks sparkly tonight.

I wonder what's really going on up there.

A kid

Another kid

WE HAVE LIFT-OFF!

How big is space?

Is it noisy?

Is it smelly?

What are stars, moons and planets anyway?

What does it feel like to travel into space?

Charlie, an expert on everything, especially space pongs and puzzling planets

SPACE STARTS HERE!

Around the Earth there is a blanket of air called the atmosphere. It stretches up and up, getting thinner and thinner. Space starts about 100 kilometres (62 miles) high, where the air runs out.

WOOHOO!

It takes three or four minutes for a rocket to reach space from Earth.

The place where space starts is called the Kármán Line.

Kármán Line

100 kilometres (62 miles)

Earth

The atmosphere, made of air that humans can breathe. Hurrah!

Space starts here

Empty-looking parts of space are not always empty. There are sometimes gases and tiny grains of dust floating around.

Space is mostly very cold, but the nearer you get to a star, the hotter it gets.

Space and all the things in it are called the universe. We don't know how far it stretches and we can't see all of it.

It's thought the universe was born about 13.7 billion years ago.

There could be around 200 billion trillion stars, just in the part of the universe we can see.

SPACE IS BIG!

IS SPACE SMELLY? IS IT NOISY?

Astronauts who have come back from spacewalking have noticed a smell on their spacesuits. It reminded them of burning metal or burnt nuts. It might be the smell of space dust.

Inside a spaceship it usually smells of astronaut sweat and farts – like a bedroom that's never had the window opened.

★ THE ★
SPACESHIP SMELLY
★ ★ ★

PARP!

We know that there are smelly chemicals in some parts of space. For instance, gases on the planet Uranus smell of stinky rotten eggs. A cloud of dust and gas called Sagittarius B2 is made of chemicals that probably smell like raspberries!

Could you be a space sniffer? The US space organization NASA has a team of top smellers to test everything they put in a new spaceship. Anything that's too pongy gets taken out.

Sound is made when tiny air molecules in the Earth's atmosphere vibrate (shake) and your ear detects the vibrating.

Far out in empty space there are hardly any molecules, so there's no sound. There will be sounds on planets that have an atmosphere, though.

WHIRR, CLONK!

I heard that!

On Mars the atmosphere is thin, so noises probably sound extra-quiet. On Venus, where the atmosphere is thick, noises probably sound like they are being made underwater.

It can be quite noisy inside a spaceship because of all the whirring, rumbling equipment.

MEET THE STARS

Stars aren't actually star-shaped. They are gigantic balls of super-hot burning gas.

Our Sun is bigger than most stars, but there are much bigger ones, too. The biggest discovered so far is more than 1,700 times bigger than our Sun.

When we look up at stars, they seem to twinkle. That's because the light they give out wobbles as it comes through our atmosphere.

I'm burning to meet you!

The Sun is our nearest star. The next closest star to us would take thousands of years to reach in a fast rocket.

Stars are different colours, depending on how hot they are. They might be shades of blue, yellow, orange or red.

When the most massive stars come to the end of their long lives, they explode and send stardust across the universe. In fact, some stardust lands on Earth every day!

This is all hot stuff!

You will see different stars through the year. They seem to move because the Earth is always moving through space, spinning round the Sun.

Long ago, people looked up at the stars and imagined joining them up, like dot-to-dot pictures, to make imaginary shapes called constellations. They have names such as the Bear, the Crab and the Lion.

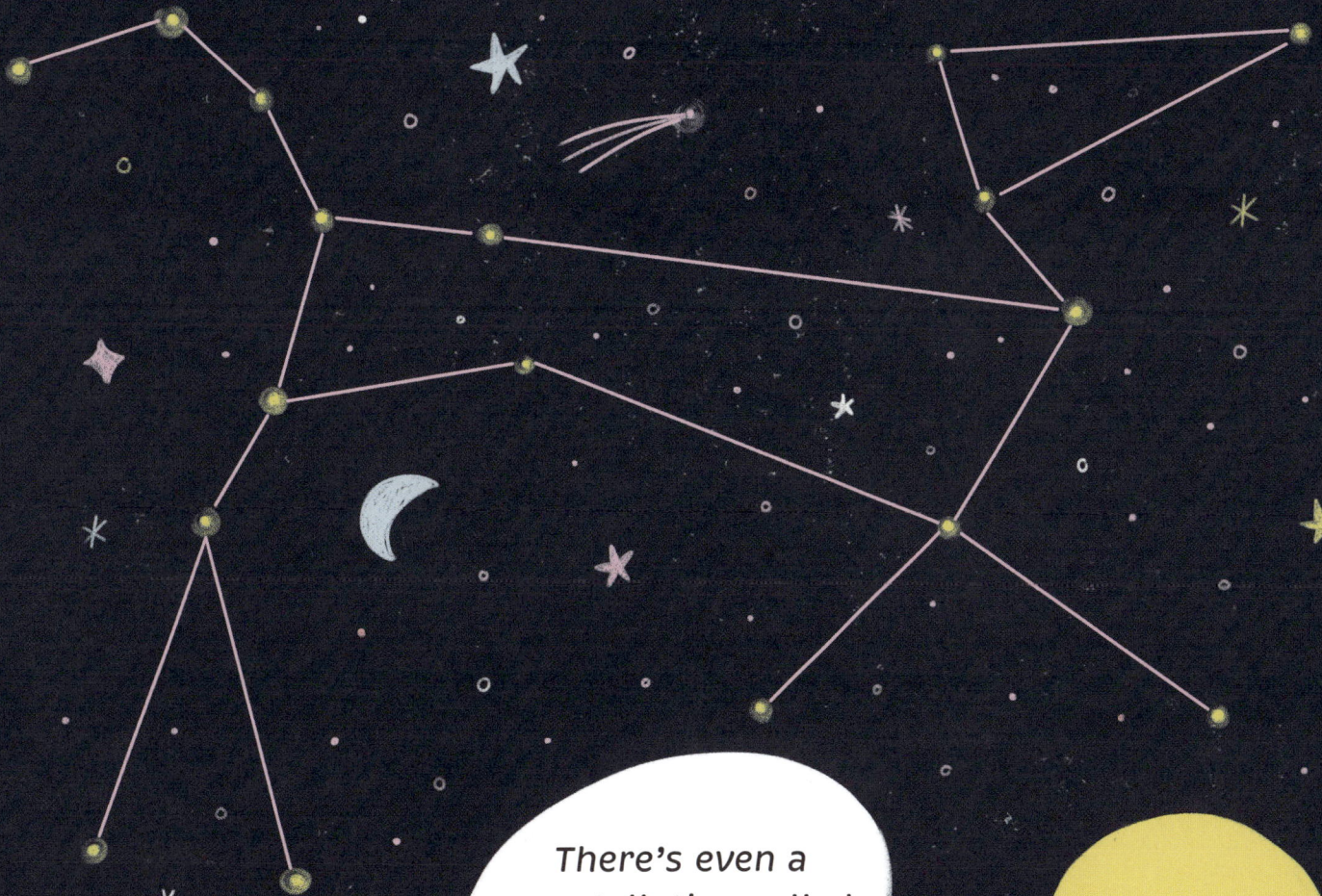

There's even a constellation called the Big Dog.

Now that's a star pooch!

WHEN THE SUN BURPS!

The Sun is 149 million kilometres (93 million miles) away from Earth. It takes 8 minutes and 20 seconds for its light to reach us.

The Sun is so big that 1.3 million Earths would fit inside it.

The surface of the Sun is about five times hotter than the hottest volcano lava on Earth.

The Sun is spotty! It has some slightly cooler dark patches called sunspots on its surface.

BU

Sometimes a burst of super-hot energy comes out of the Sun, like a gigantic burp. It's called a solar flare.

Occasionally the Sun gets busy and sends out several flares a week. At other times it stays quiet and sends out roughly one a week that can be detected from Earth.

Really big solar flares can sometimes mess up radio signals on Earth, but they don't happen very often.

RP!

NEVER LOOK DIRECTLY AT THE SUN. It would damage your eyes.

A RIDE INSIDE
THE MILKY WAY

Our Sun and Earth are part of a galaxy – a huge group of stars and planets that spin around in space together. Our galaxy is called the Milky Way.

From above, it looks like a spinning blob with arms whirling out from the middle, rather like water spinning down a plughole.

WHOOSH!

All the stars that you can see are in the Milky Way. There are trillions of other galaxies in the universe, but we can only see three of them with our naked eye. Many more can be seen using a powerful telescope.

WHIZZ!

Most new stars are born in the spiral arms.

The middle of the Milky Way looks like a bulge.

WHEEEE!

We use light, the fastest thing we know, to measure huge distances in space. A light year is the distance light travels in one year – 9.5 trillion kilometres (6 trillion miles). The Milky Way measures about 100,000 light years across.

Our galaxy is called the Milky Way because, from Earth, we can see a part of it that looks like milk spilled across the sky. It has other names around the world, such as the Silver River or the Bird's Path.

MEET THE PLANETS

A planet is a large ball shape that orbits – goes round and round – a star. There are eight planets zooming round our Sun. Some are rocky and others are mostly wrapped in clouds of gas. Some are hot enough to melt metal and others are way colder than a freezer!

Together, the planets, the Sun, and lots of smaller objects are called the solar system.

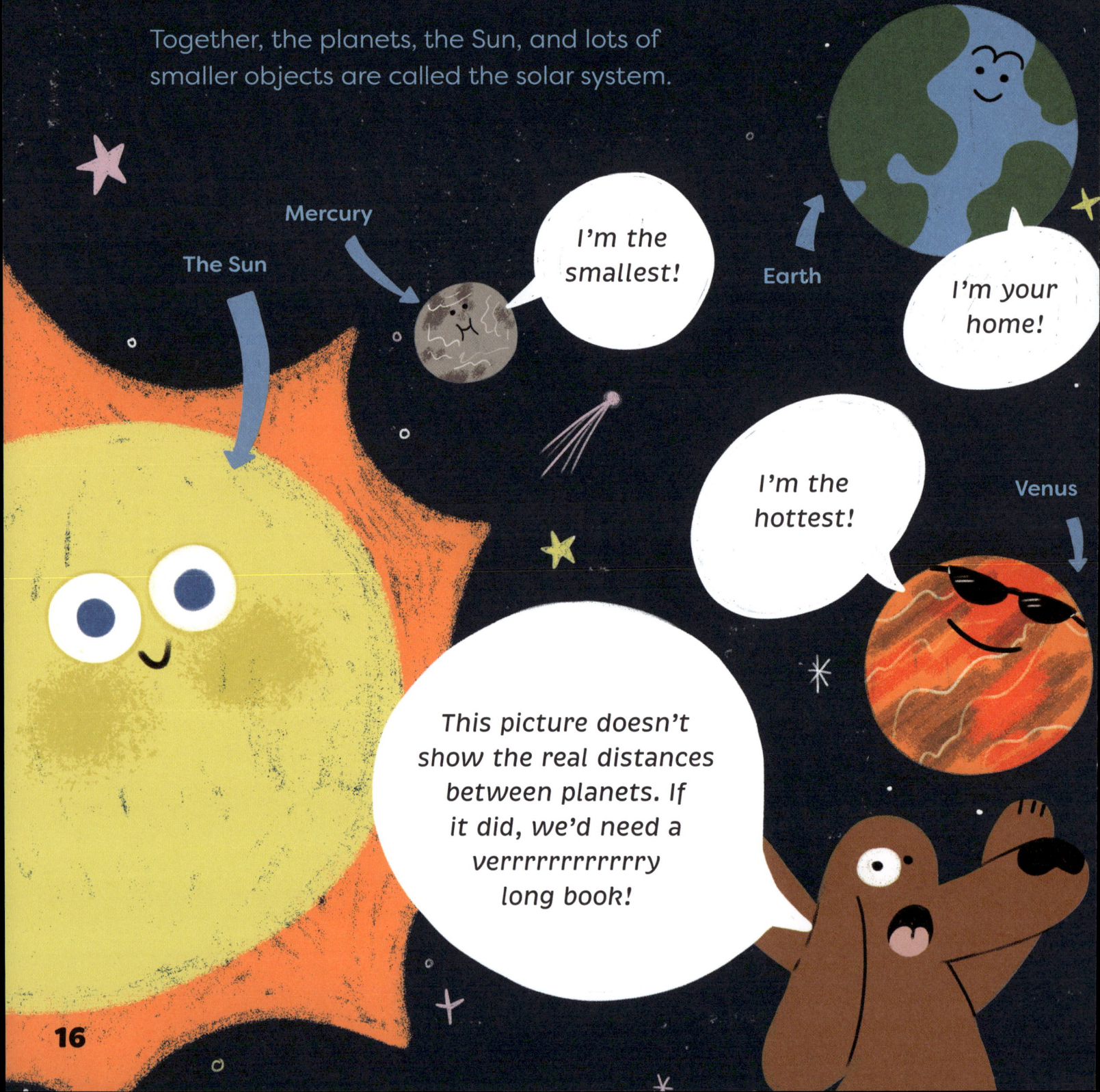

Mercury

The Sun

I'm the smallest!

Earth

I'm your home!

I'm the hottest!

Venus

This picture doesn't show the real distances between planets. If it did, we'd need a verrrrrrrrrry long book!

Long ago, people thought that the starry sky was a painted ceiling.

THESE PLANETS ROCK!

Meet the four rocky planets in the solar system and choose one to visit. (Clue: you're already on a lovely one!)

HI, MERCURY!

Mercury is 70 per cent metal. It's roasting hot on one side and super cold on the other side.

I won't visit this one.

Space-suit yourself!

HOLA, VENUS!

It's hot enough to melt lead on Venus, and it has an atmosphere of thick, poisonous gases.

I think I'll stay away.

Grrrrrr!

HEY, EARTH!

Earth has plenty of water and it's great for animals and plants because it isn't too hot or too cold. It's not perfectly round, by the way. It's shaped more like a grapefruit – fat around the middle and flatter on the top and bottom.

HuRRAH!

Earth is the only planet we know of that has life.

WOTCHA, MARS!

Mars has a dry, cold surface covered in red dust. It has water, but it's mostly hidden deep underground. It also has some caves that might make a good spot for a space base one day (more about that later!).

It would take about nine months for a rocket to get from Earth to Mars.

Nearly there!

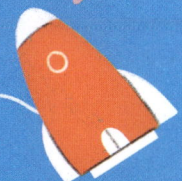

THE GASSY GANG

The solar system has four planets made mostly of gas. They're called the gas giants. You wouldn't be able to stand on any of them.

HI, JUPITER!

Jupiter is covered by gases, some of which stink. They are blown around the planet by super-strong winds. A gigantic storm, three times as big as Earth, rages there.

G'DAY, SATURN!

Saturn is covered in a thick blanket of different-coloured gases. It has lots of rings made of icy or rocky chunks whirling round and round it. It's incredibly stormy and windy, too.

Saturn – 9 times wider than Earth

Super stormy!

Jupiter – 11 times wider than Earth

Smells of wee and rotten eggs

BONJOUR, URANUS!

Uranus is mostly made of liquids, including methane, which, on Earth, is a gas. Uranus orbits on its side because another planet may once have crashed into it and knocked it over.

AHOY, NEPTUNE!

Neptune is also mostly made of liquids. It's very dark and gloomy, and it has the strongest winds in the solar system. They can reach 2,100 kilometres per hour (1,300 miles per hour)!

Uranus – 4 times wider than Earth

Neptune – 4 times wider than Earth

Smells of farts

Gloomy and gassy!

LOOK OUT! THERE'S MORE!

There's a ring of floating rocks zooming around between Mars and Jupiter. It's called the Asteroid Belt, and it contains millions of rocky lumps.

JUPITER

MARS

Hey, Jupiter! Does that belt hold up your trousers?

Watch it, Tiny!

Asteroid Belt

Out past Neptune, there's another floating ring of rock and ice, called the Kuiper Belt. A few of its rocks, such as Pluto, are big enough to be called dwarf planets.

Pluto is too small to be called a true planet.

Not fair!

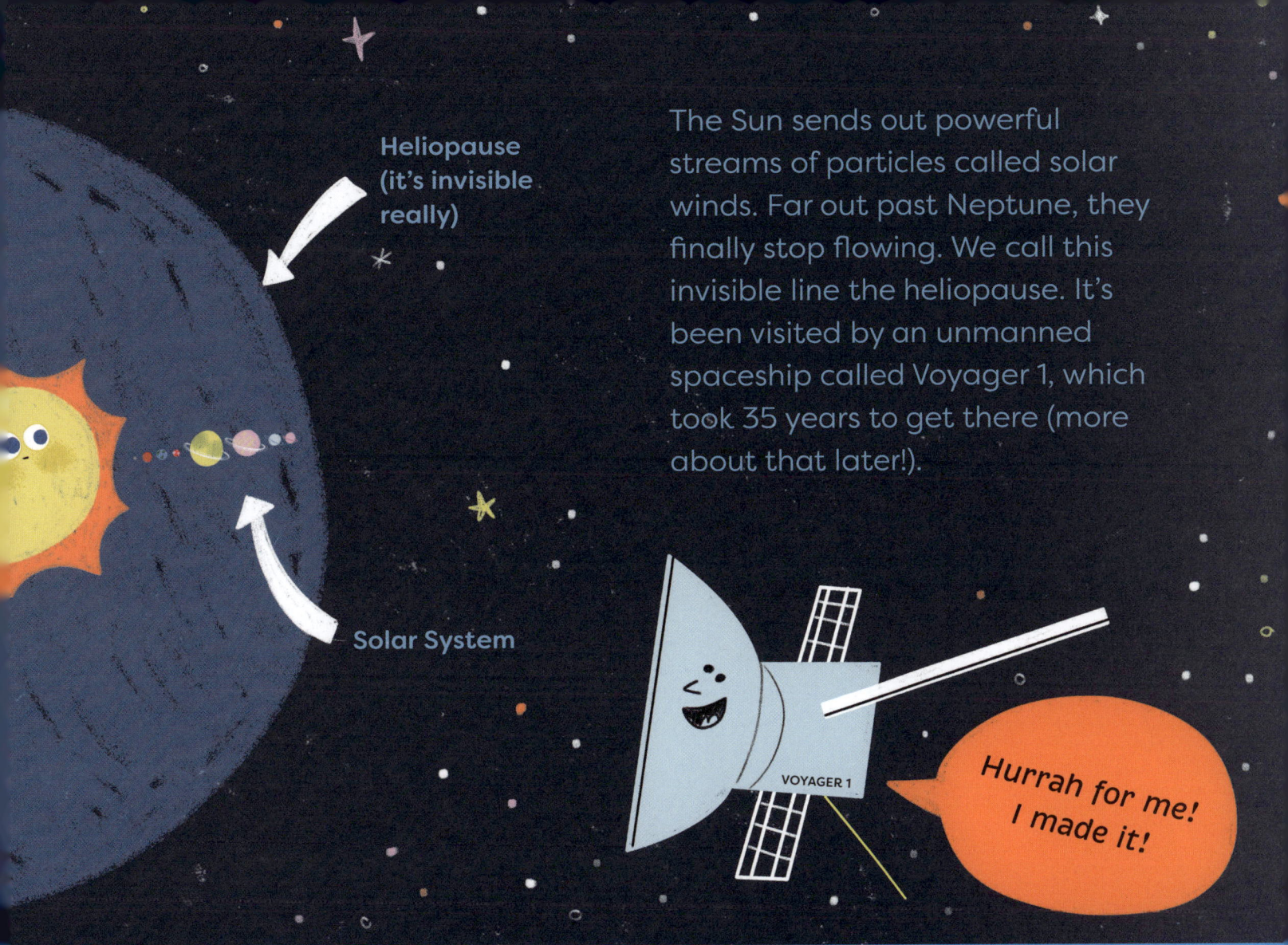

The Sun sends out powerful streams of particles called solar winds. Far out past Neptune, they finally stop flowing. We call this invisible line the heliopause. It's been visited by an unmanned spaceship called Voyager 1, which took 35 years to get there (more about that later!).

Solar System

VOYAGER 1

Hurrah for me! I made it!

Far out beyond everything else, there's a gigantic cloud of icy lumps called the Oort Cloud. The ice lumps are called comets (see page 30). It would take hundreds of years to get to the Oort Cloud, even for a spaceship at top speed.

It's like a cloud of giant whizzing ice lollies!

MEET THE MOONS

A moon is an object that goes round and round a planet. We know there are nearly 300 moons in the solar system – and there might be more we haven't found yet.

ZOOM!

No two moons are the same.

Just like us!

WHOOSH!

In our solar system, there is one volcanic moon. Jupiter's moon, Io, has hundreds of volcanoes and giant lakes of boiling lava. Some of its lava shoots up high into space.

BRRRR!

Some moons are icy places. Jupiter's moon Europa has an icy crust, though it also has a hidden ocean underneath. Giant plumes of water sometimes burst out through the ice and shoot up, like mega-fountains.

OUCH!

Moons often get battered by asteroids. Jupiter's moon, Callisto, is the most heavily bashed-about moon we know. It's got so many craters it looks as if it's covered in spots!

SPLASH!

Moons can be surprising and strange. Saturn's moon, Titan, has rain, but its atmosphere is so thick that the raindrops probably fall in slow-motion – six times slower than they do on Earth.

MEET THE
BEST MOON
(OURS!)

There's one moon that we can easily see because it's going round and round us. It's the one and only silvery Moon!

THE MOON...

...doesn't make any light itself. It reflects light from the Sun.

...looks as if it has dark and light patches. The dark patches are flat plains and the light patches are higher ground.

...is covered in rubble and dust. There's probably some ice in a few of the deep craters.

...doesn't have weather such as wind or rain. It can get very cold or very hot, though.

Only a few people have walked on the Moon so far. They've left behind lots of bits and pieces – including 12 pairs of boots, 2 golf balls, a falcon bird feather, 3 space buggies and around 96 bags of sick, wee and poo!

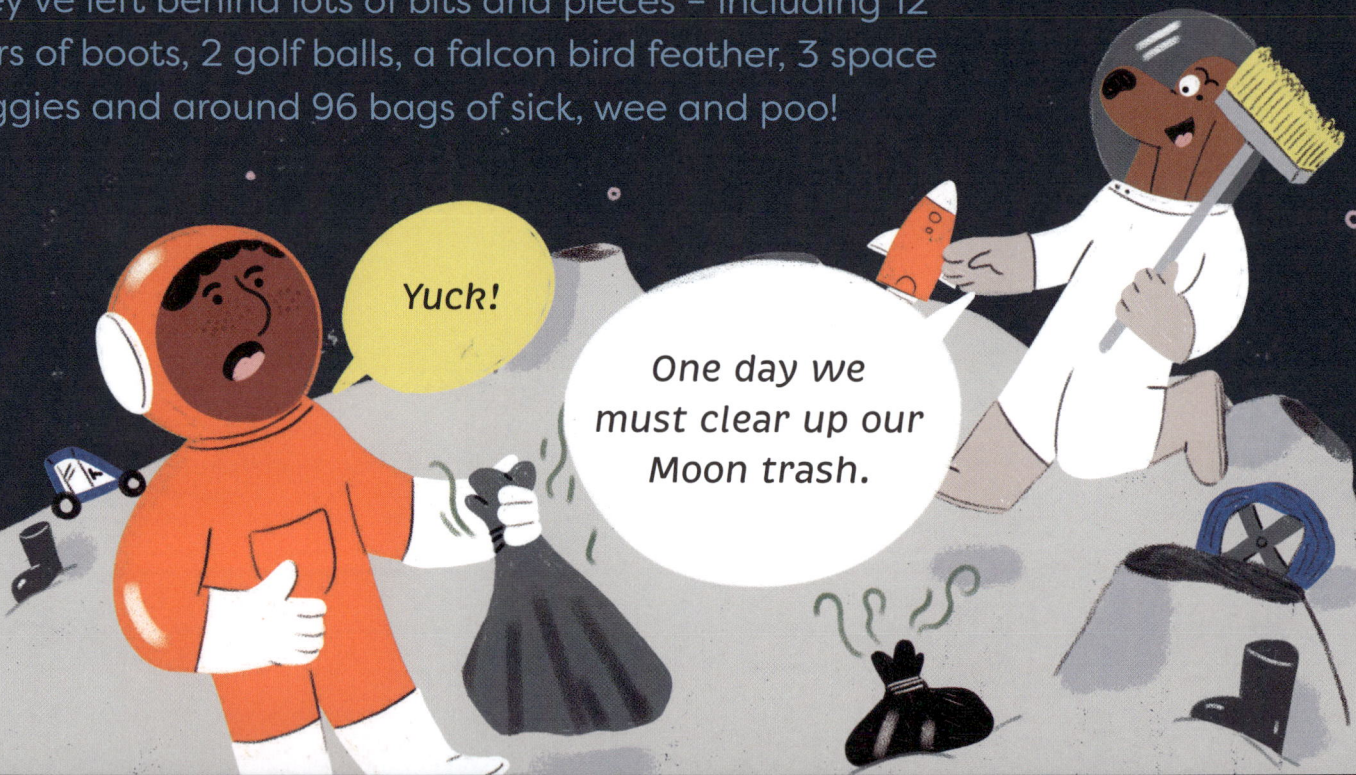

Yuck!

One day we must clear up our Moon trash.

MOON MOVES

To us, the Moon looks as though it slowly changes shape each month, from a crescent to a disc and back again. It's not really changing, though. The shape you see is the part lit up by the Sun, which changes as the Moon travels round Earth. Watch out for these shapes, called Moon phases.

Crescent Moon

Quarter Moon

Looking good, Moon!

Gibbous Moon

Full Moon

RIDE WITH THE ASTEROIDS

Asteroids are lumps of rock floating in space. There are millions of them whizzing round the Sun in the Asteroid Belt between Mars and Jupiter. Some are as small as boulders and others are more like mini planets.

What are you called?

Rocky!

Some asteroids even have their own mini moons.

Unmanned spacecraft have flown round some asteroids, taking photos. A few of them have even managed to land and bring samples of asteroid rock back to Earth.

Hi there!

Asteroids come in all sorts of shapes, including ones that look like giant, lumpy space potatoes, dog bones and sausages.

CRASH MISSION!

Sometimes asteroids slip out of the Asteroid Belt and hurtle towards the Sun. It's rare that they come near Earth, but we are planning ways to push them away if they do. In 2022, as a test, a spacecraft called DART crashed into a small asteroid and changed the way it moved.

BAM!

Oi!

CHASE A COMET

Wow! What's that streaking across the sky? It's a comet zooming past Earth as it orbits round the Sun. Comets are visitors from the faraway regions of the solar system.

Gas tail

A comet has two tails.

WHIZZ!

Dust tail

Some comet tails stretch up to a million kilometres.

OOOH!

The front part of a comet is a massive lump of ice, dust and rubble. When the Sun warms it up, some of the dust and gas stream out behind in two long tails that glow in the sunlight.

A big comet travels past Earth every 5 to 10 years. Smaller ones go past every year or two.

SPARKLE!

AHHH!

In 2014 and 2016, two spacecraft, called Rosetta and Philae, landed on a lumpy comet called 67P, shaped a bit like a giant bath duck. They are still riding on it now, zooming through space!

IT'S STRANGE IN OUTER SPACE!

Planets in other solar systems are very hard to spot, though there are probably trillions. We have found around 5,000 so far. Meet a few of the most amazing!

HD 189733 b

This blue gas giant probably has glass raindrops. Ouch!

K2-18b

This planet is covered in ocean so super hot that it's probably mostly steam.

Which one would you like to visit?

Newly discovered planets are given boring names made up of letters and numbers. Later they get given more fun names.

HUMANS...
LAUNCH!

It's very difficult for humans to travel into space.
So far, we've orbited the Earth and visited the Moon.

Astronauts are up here, sitting in their spacecraft. They're going to visit a space station orbiting Earth.

To get above the Earth's atmosphere, a spacecraft must be attached to a powerful rocket full of fuel.

The rocket needs to reach a speed over 28,000 kilometres per hour (17,000 miles per hour) to overcome the gravity (the pull) of Earth.

It will take 8 to 11 minutes to reach orbit. Then the spacecraft will separate from the rocket.

When the rocket's fuel is set alight, gases blast out of its engine nozzles and push it upwards. The gases get so hot they would easily melt iron!

BOOM!

3...2...1... BLAST-OFF!

The astronauts sit strapped inside their spaceship. Everything shakes and rattles around them as the massive rocket engines fire.

As they zoom upwards, they feel lots of pushing pressure – called G-force. It makes them feel as if they are being squashed by heavy weights.

Once the rockets are switched off the pressure disappears and everything feels floaty.

Are we nearly there yet?

We have lift-off!

Experts control the rocket from Earth. They work in a building called Mission Control.

EAT, WEE AND SLEEP IN SPACE

Living in a space station isn't like living at home on Earth. Astronauts are weightless up there and everything floats!

Floating around all day won't give you much exercise. You'll need to work out in the space gym for a couple of hours a day to keep your muscles and bones healthy.

You'll need to be strapped into your exercise machine so you don't float away.

Yum! Space food!

Food comes in pouches and tubes. Bread is banned because of floating crumbs, but tortillas are allowed.

The space toilet will suck away your poo and wee like a vacuum cleaner. The wee gets cleaned and recycled into drinking water. The poo gets bagged up and destroyed, or sometimes it's taken back to Earth for scientists to study.

A PRESENT FROM SPACE

Poo

Because you're floating, you need to sleep strapped to the wall of the space station.

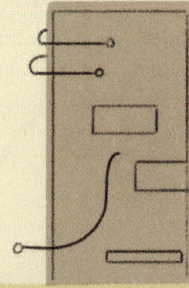

It's out-of-this-world up here!

It's important to relax and stay happy onboard. You might want to play your own music, read books or chat to your friends and family back on Earth.

You'll need to work while you're out in space. There are lots of science experiments to do, such as seeing how plants grow in space and how small animals such as insects and spiders cope living up there with you.

Wow! Spiders can weave webs in space.

Wow! Humans look so funny floating around!

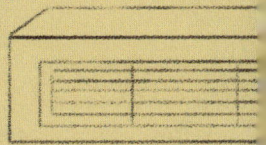

WHAT'S THAT MOVING LIGHT?

Back on Earth, on a clear night, you might see small lights moving slowly and steadily across the sky. Are they alien spaceships? No. They're probably satellites!

Satellites are machines that orbit Earth, sending and receiving signals.

I help you watch your favourite show.

A **communications satellite** sends and receives TV and radio signals, bouncing them around the planet and into your home.

Dish for receiving signals

An **Earth observation satellite** measures and photographs all kinds of things on Earth, such as forests and oceans.

I help look after the planet.

There are nearly 10,000 satellites orbiting Earth.

A **weather satellite** measures and watches all the weather going on down below.

Rain's on its way!

Communications antennae

Solar panels for power

An **astronomical satellite** looks out at other stars and planets.

Hiya, Saturn!

Your car might get my signals.

A **navigation satellite** sends signals to help people work out exactly where they are on Earth.

Some of them go round up to 16 times a day.

They don't have their own lights, but they shine when they reflect sunlight.

ROBOTS...
LAUNCH!

Robot machines called probes travel into outer space and send back all sorts of information about what they find.

In 1977, two probes – Voyager 1 and Voyager 2 – left Earth to travel through the solar system. They have sent back lots of information about the planets they passed, and they're still flying, on and on, into deep space!

I'm off. Byeee!

Wake up, probe!

Wotcha, Jupiter!

Scientists back on Earth can send signals to a space probe to change its direction or make it work differently.

Sometimes probes are sent to orbit planets. One of these is Juno, which is zooming round Jupiter sending back lots of amazing pictures.

The ACE probe didn't zoom off into outer space. Instead, it went towards the Sun and keeps a watch on what's going on there. It can let us know when solar flares happen (see page 12).

It's always sunny up here!

HELLO FROM EARTH!

Voyager 1 and 2 are carrying records full of information about Earth. If space aliens ever find and play them, they will hear all sorts of Earth noises, including:

- animal noises, such as whale song and bird song

- human noises, such as footsteps and laughter

- music from around the world

- natural sounds, such as waves crashing and thunder rolling.

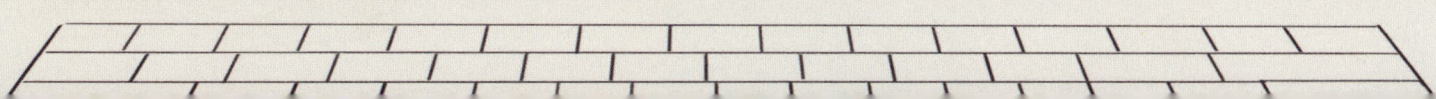

SEEING INTO SPACE

We need telescopes to see a long way into space. Lenses or mirrors inside a telescope collect the light from stars far away. They focus it into a picture for us.

The James Webb Telescope out in space

Gold-plated mirrors

It's amazing out there!

A small telescope on Earth

The size of a school bus

Space telescopes can be sent into orbit to get an extra-clear view of space. They have sent back pictures of incredible events such as stars exploding and galaxies crashing into each other.

The light that we see coming from space has travelled a long, long way and taken ages to arrive. The James Webb Space Telescope spotted Earendel, the furthest star ever found. Its light took 12.9 billion years to reach us!

All sorts of new stars and planets are out here.

This smudge could be a faraway galaxy.

It's thought the universe was born 13.7 billion years ago, and so far the James Webb Space Telescope has detected light that was made 13.5 billion years ago. That's back near the beginning of time!

Radio telescopes on the ground listen in to space. They have giant metal dishes that collect different sorts of signals made by stars. The measurements can tell us all sorts of things, such as when stars were born and how big they are.

Dish as big as 30 football pitches

The biggest radio telescope in the world is in China. It's called FAST.

WHERE ARE THE SPACE ALIENS?

We don't yet know if there is any life in other parts of space. There are trillions and trillions of planets, though, so the chances are high.

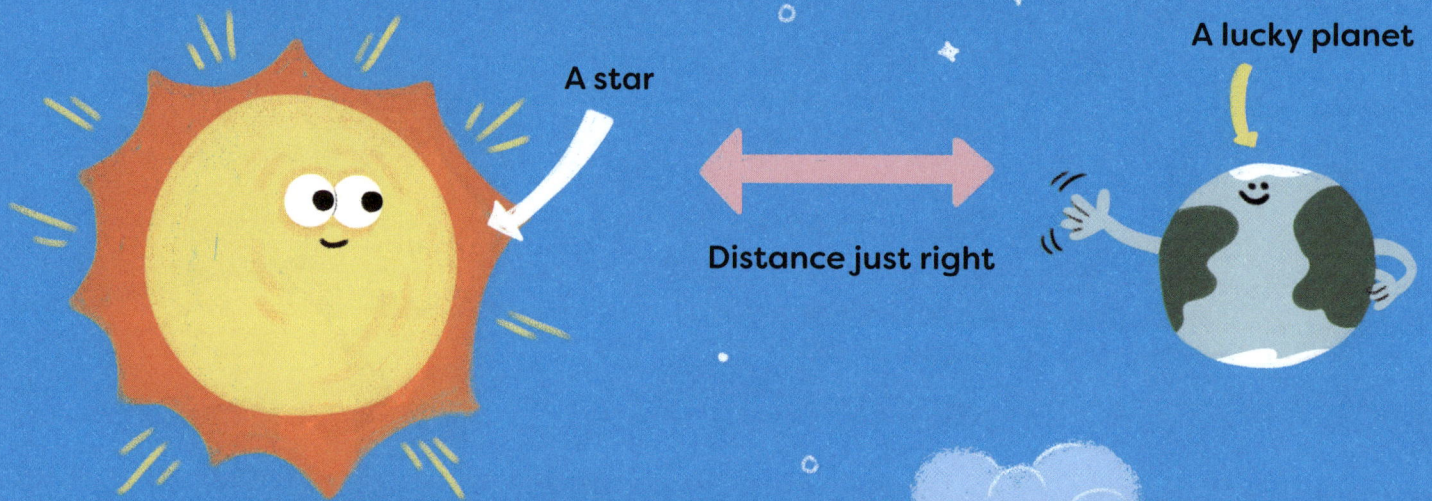

A star

A lucky planet

Distance just right

To support life, a planet must be just the right distance away from a star for water to survive as a liquid. We call this perfect distance the Goldilocks Zone, after the tale of *Goldilocks and the Three Bears*. In the story, Goldilocks tried three bowls of porridge.

One bowl was too hot.

One bowl was too cold.

One bowl was just right!

Our Earth is just right for life. We're in the Goldilocks Zone!

CALLING SPACE! CALLING SPACE!

We've been monitoring space for a while to pick up radio signals that might have been sent by aliens. We haven't heard any yet, though.

Nobody knows what alien life might look like. It could be tiny bacteria, or it might look more like us. What do you think?

They could go on space walkies!

I wonder if there are dogs on other planets?

WELCOME TO OUR SPACE BASE

There are exciting plans for the future in space, including bases on the Moon and Mars. Perhaps you'll visit them one day! What do you think your base might look like?

Air supply inside

Super-tough tyres for driving over rocks and craters

Calling base. I'm on my way!

Mobile science lab in the back

You'll be able to drive around in a space rover. Inside, there will be air to breathe – like a mini spaceship on wheels.

Nobody can walk outside without wearing a spacesuit and helmet, and carrying an air supply to breathe.

Air supply pack

Robots will probably be sent to build space bases and do lots of work around them.

Busy robots

A base might need to be hidden in underground caves to protect it from meteoroid strikes and dangerous energy rays from the Sun.

Astronauts will need to grow their food indoors, using seeds from Earth.

Let's zoom to the Moon soon!

Now we know that space is ace!

Inside the base it will feel more like being on Earth, with separate rooms for sleeping, eating and working.

47

I hope you enjoyed this book full of space! Think of me next time you look up at the twinkly night sky. **Woof!**

First published in 2026 by Happy Yak, an imprint of The Quarto Group.
1 Triptych Place, London,
SE1 9SH, United Kingdom.
T (0)20 7700 6700 F (0)20 7700 8066
www.quarto.com

EEA Representation, WTS Tax d.o.o., Žanova ulica 3, 4000 Kranj, Slovenia.
www.wts-tax.si

Senior Commissioning Editor: Carly Madden
Senior Designer: Mike Henson
Editor: Laura Knowles

Consultant: Mike Goldsmith
Creative Director: Malena Stojić
Associate Publisher: Rhiannon Findlay
Senior Production Controller: Elizabeth Reardon

A catalogue record for this book is available from the British Library.

ISBN: 978 1 8360 0213 0

9 8 7 6 5 4 3 2 1

Manufactured in Huizhou, Guangdong, China TT092025

FSC
www.fsc.org
MIX
Paper | Supporting
responsible forestry
FSC® C016973